100 Aphorisms

And Words To Live By

Selected By

Richard J. Halpern

Design Director:
Armond Saidai

Richard J. Halpern

Has a degree in journalism, Is a World War II veteran, has spent 32 years on the business staff of Ziff Davis Publishing Company working primarily with Popular Electronics, Electronic World, and Stereo Review. He has two daughters, six grandsons, and five great-grandchildren. He is the author of "Portraits- A Visual Map of Who We Are" that depicts Port Washington, New York persons who make a singular contribution to the well-being of the community.

Armond Saidai

Is the collaborator and design director on 100 Aphorisms.
Born in London is a graduate of Pratt Institute. He has worked as a designer in New York City and and has been locally involved in design projects as well as businesses in which he has sponsored numerous cultural events for Port Washington, New York artists.

SPECIAL RECOGNITION

To those individuals who consented to read a first

draft of '100 Aphorisms' and pick out their

favorite one- thank you.

You're in appropriate places and your comments

were striking and helpful.

Your reaction assisted me in seeing the

universality of this effort. **

** To all readers: I would appreciate a personal comment on your favorite Aphorism for possible inclusion in a future edition. Contact us at : Portraits1031@gmail.com.

25 years ago I began to collect "old sayings" that appealed to me. 25 years later I have picked these out of the pile.

You can call it a personal philosophy or purely personal prejudices, but I see these words as beyond sayings.

Some are goals that seem difficult to attain; others are reachable and sensible.

Judge for yourself.

ACKNOWLEDGMENTS

To Juliet, my late wife, for her wisdom and common sense.

To Mel Gordon, for his insight and fine mind.

To Kate Wilson, for her reading and her comments.

To Leo Hollisher, for his printing and publishing prowess.

To Martin Star, for his computer savvy and assistance.

To my daughters, Shari and Mara, for their special ideas and efforts.

You gave wings to my imagination.

Table of Contents

ACTION

Every Public action, when it is
not customary, either is wrong,
or, if it is right, is a dangerous precedent.
It follows that nothing should ever be done
for the first time.

Francis Macdonald Cornford

(1874-1943)

An English classical scholar and poet. He was a
professor of ancient philosophy at Trinity college
and was elected a fellow of the British empire
in 1937.

Jacques Louis David

ACTION

The Distance is nothing. It's only the first step that's important.

Marquise du Deffand

(1697-1782)

A woman of letters. A leading figure of French society where she held court for a long period of time.

If I had not stopped to measure the distance; if I had taken the first step; would I have found what was important?

Bette Baum
Riverdale, New York

When you want to accomplish something, don't spend too much time contemplating whether you can or cannot succeed. Once you take the first step you are already one step closer to achieving your goal. It is then you will realize it will soon be within reach and that you are capable of accomplishing anything.

Barry Levine
Great Neck, New York

ACTION

One never notices what has been done; one can only see what remains to be done.

Marie Curie

(1867-1934)

Was a Polish born physicist and chemist famous for her work on radioactivity.

It is difficult, yet important, to remember that we
all work in negative space—whether it is the
judgment of someone else's work or our own.
A good leader will always make it a point to
recognize and appreciate the good work that
someone has done instead of only recognizing
that which still remains to be finished.
This is easier said than done, but these words of
wisdom were shared with me at the early stages of
my career, and have served me very well so far in
becoming an effective leader.

Steven Berger
Pasadena , California

ACTION

Only those who risk going too far can possibly find out how far one can go.

T. S. Eliot

(1888-1965)

He was an American born English poet, playwright and literary critic, arguably the most important English language poet of the 20 th century.

I have always liked this quote in the office when we undertake what appears to be a huge or near impossible project. A similar quote from Andre Gide,"one does not discover new lands without consenting to lose sight of the shore for a very long time." Always makes me think of Columbus, Magellan, astronauts.

Bob Halpern-Givens

Crystal Lake, Illinois

ART

The true function of the artist is not to express *himself*, but to express his vision of the world; and most modern art is sterile because the artist places himself in the center of the world, as the observed rather than as the observer.

Source Unknown

Wassily Kandinsky

ART

The path to fulfillment_and every so often to money and to greatness_ begins with the realization that the artist has only to please him or herself.

Frank Van Riper

He served for two decades in the New York Daily News Washington bureau. He was an award winning White House correspondent, a national political correspondent and Washington bureau news editor.

Jean-Léon Gérôme

ART

Art has never been, and never will be, democratic. The counting of noses may decide elections, but it cannot decide merit. From ballads to baseball players, the untrained amateur always chooses wrong. And when book publishers and movie producers decide to give the public 'what it wants' they may call it 'democracy' but its real name is older and shorter__ avarice

Sydney J. Harris

(1917-1986)

Was an American journalist for the Chicago Daily News and later for the Chicago Sun_Times.

Pierre Auguste Renoir

ART

If art doesn't make us better, then what on earth is it for?

Alice Walker

(1944 -)

She is an African American author and poet, best known for the novel 'The Color Purple.

Leonardo Da Vinci

CHOICES

Profound human suffering must take preference over political expediency.

Source Unknown

Anyone with a conscience, a heart or empathy must believe this and act on it. What a beautiful world if it could be.

Dan Simon

Port Washington, New York

CHOICES

If other people are going to talk, conversation becomes impossible.

James Abbott McNeill Whistler

(1834-1903)

An American born English based artist, his art was characterized by a subtle delicacy, while his public personality was combative.

Was Whistler thinking of restaurants these days? When the noise level of conversation rises at places in which we eat, it literally and figuratively hits the ceiling.

What happened to quiet dining? The soaring sound level makes it impossible to enjoy conversation whether it be Whistler's or anyone elses.

Marie S. Rautenberg
Port Washington, New York

COURAGE

Nothing great can get done--or be resisted--
without courage.

Source Unknown

Rembrandt Peale

COURAGE

It is the fear of being called a coward that makes most men courageous in a crisis; but real courage, which is rare, consists in doing what you know is right, regardless of what men call you.

Source Unknown

Choosing to not follow a crowd is sometimes a difficult thing to do, but the rewards of knowing you did the right thing is priceless. I strive to show my children this in my everyday actions.

Louna Suberro

Brooklyn, New York

COURAGE

Every man has the right to risk his own life in order to save it.

Jean-Jacques Rousseau

(1712-1778)

A major Genevan (Switzerland) philosopher, writer and composer of 18 th century Romanticism.

Eugene Delacroix

COURAGE

Everyone has talent. What is rare is the courage to follow the talent to the dark place where it leads.

Erica Jong

(1942 -)

An American author and teacher. She is best known for her fiction and poetry.

Albert Edelfelt

CRITICISM

To speak ill of others is a dishonest way of praising ourselves.

Will Durant

(*1885-1981*)

A prolific writer, historian and philosopher best know for "The Story of Civilization."

CRITICISM

You can spot a bad critic when he starts by discussing the poet and not the poem.

Ezra Pound

(1885-1972)

He was an American expatriate and critic. Pound helped to discover and shaped the work of T.S. Eliot, James Joyce, Robert Frost and Ernest Hemingway. A Fascist and an Anti-Semite he was indicted as a traitor. His political views insure that his work will remain controversial.

Poetry is an art that moves, Criticism can only just try and approach it. A man like Ezra Pound, who had a very interesting life, is right when he says criticize my poem, not me.

Ariel Basom

Seattle, Washington

CRITICISM

Hating anything in the way of illnatured gossip ourselves, we are always grateful to those who do it for us.

Saki (H.H. Munro)

(1870-1960)

A British writer whose witty and sometimes macabre stories satirized Edwardian society and culture.

Shinsue ito

DESTINY

What we anticipate seldom occurs: what we least expect generally happens.

Benjamin Disraeli

(1804-1881)

He was a British Prime Minister, a parliamentarian, a conservative statesman and literary figure. His religion was Judaism until he was thirteen and entered the Church of England. A prominent historian supports evidence that he was a 'Marrano.'

EGO

They looked into each other's eyes; he saw himself, she saw herself.

Source Unknown

It was my first adult relationship. I moved out to the West Coast for a boy, thinking that having recently graduated this would be a wonderful start to my real life.

The relationship itself fell apart within months having mostly been based on our own egos rather than each other. We looked at each other, but not into each other. Looking back, I learned the most about myself from that experience and wouldn't trade it for the world.

Emmelia Halpern-Givens
Chicago, Illinois

EXAMPLE

Example is not the main thing in influencing

others. It is the only thing.

Albert Schweitzer

(1875-1965)

He was a Franco-German (Alsatian) theologian,

organist, philosopher, physician and medical missionary.

Claude Oscar Monet

FAITH

It's not dying for faith that's so hard, it's living up to it.

William Makepeace Thackeray

(1811-1863)

He was an English novelist of the 19 th century and was famous for his satirical works.

Jean-Léon Gérôme

FAITH

Absolute faith corrupts as absolute power corrupts.

Eric Hoffer

(1902-1983)

A longshoreman, he was an American social writer and philosopher.

FREEDOM

The last of the human freedoms is to choose one's attitude in any given set of circumstances, to choose one's own way.

Viktor Frankl

(1905-1997)

He was an Austrian neurologist and psychiatrist, as well as a Holocaust survivor. His best known work was 'Man's Search For Meaning.'

Whether our attitude is shouted out to the world or kept quietly in our heart and soul it is ours and has great effect on who we are and how we exist in the world. Not choosing and giving someone else power over your life, your attitude is still a choice you make.

Emery Hurst Mikel. Huntington,New York

In life I have found that these circumstances offer a route by which to navigate our way. Sometimes lost, with no signs or maps we learn to adapt and find our own path, our own road.

Jesse Halpern, Busan, South Korea

I realized I have felt stressed or happy in both highs or lows in career, marriage and parenthood. Why can I feel either way in the same conditions? It has come down to choice. What I find challenging is how to develop the habit of making the choice to be happy despite conditions, ego or emotions. That is something to continue to strive for in the future.

Jonas Basom, Culver City, California

In life I have found that these circum- stances
offer a route by which to navigate our way.
Sometimes lost, with designs or maps we learn
to adapt and find our own path, our own road.

Jesse Halpern, Pusan, South Korea

This aphorism reflects my own work and my own
life with my desire to create positive change in
my community.. If I act with conviction and
follow the path I am determined to be on, then I
will make the change I seek. I believe that by
thinking and acting independently in my work, I
can set myself in a direction where my actions
are meaningful.
My actions are not just important to myself;
there can also be an impact on the broader
community.

Ezra Basom, Seattle, Washington

FRIENDSHIP

Close your eyes to the faults of others and watch the doors of friendship swing wide.

E. C. McKenzie

A retired minister of the Church of Christ, he served as editor in chief of the standard reference indexed Bible. He is the author of fourteen books, including "Salted Peanuts and Mixed Nuts."

I chose this aphorism because it captivated

my thoughts. It made me think of everyone

I have crossed paths with and how their

faults persuaded my decision on whether

or not our friendship would work.

Shekeva Issac

Jamaica, New York

FRIENDSHIP

A friend knows how to allow for mere quantity in your talk, and only replies to the quality.

William Dean Howells

(1837-1920)

He was an American realist author and literary critic.

William-Adolphe Bouguereau

FRIENDSHIP

I always felt that the great high privilege, relief, and comfort of friendship was that one had to explain nothing.

Katherine Mansfield

(1888-1923)

One of the world's best known short story writers and New Zealand's most famous author.

Vasily Perov

FRIENDSHIP

Friendship is unnecessary, like philosophy, like art. It has no survival value; rather it is one of those things that give value to survival.

C. S. Lewis
(1898-1963)

Born in Belfast, Ireland, he made major contributions in literary criticism, children's literature, fantasy literature, and popular thelogy that brought him international renown and acclaim.

Winslow Homer

FRIENDSHIP

We are on the wrong track when we think of friendship as some thing to get rather than something to give.

Source Unknown

Now that I am elderly, I deeply regret that I always intended to, but never did, tell those who I knew so well, how much I valued their friendship. Now, they are not here to listen.

Larry Newman

Floral Park, New York

FRIENDSHIP

We need two kinds of acquaintances,
one to complain to, while we boast
to the others.

Logan Pearsall Smith
(1865-1946)

He was an American born essayist and critic, known for his aphorisms and epigrams and his *Trivia* has been highly rated.

Gaetano Bellei

HAPPINESS

The secret of happiness is not in doing what one likes, but in liking what one has to do.

James M. Barrie

(1860-1937)

He was a Scottish author and playwright, and the author of 'Peter Pan' or 'The Boy Who Would Not Grow Up.'

I chose this quote because it conveys something that I've always believed and that is- in life- we all must learn to have versatile dispositions. We all must learn to accept and embrace the things that we have to do. Certainly, it makes life easier if we like those things.

Julian Halpern

S. Hadley, Massachusetts

HAPPINESS

The grand essentials to happiness in this life are something to do, something to love and something to hope for.

Joseph Addison

(1672-1719)

An English essayist, a poet, playwright and politician, he was a man of letters.

I have found in my own life that having the right partner to love, finding joyful employment, and believing in my dreams fuels my life with meaning and perpetual happiness.

Susan Porter

Culver City, California

HAPPINESS

If we try to grasp happiness, it always escapes us; if we try to hand it out to others, it sticks to our hands like glue.

John Marks Templeton

(1912-2008)

He was an evolutionist, pantheist and universalist. Few have done as much to promote a sense of unity among the world's religions.

Happiness has to be a natural occurrence; kindness and love may help you get to that state.

Trevor Tingle

Bronx, New York

It's my first year in college and happiness hasn't set for me yet. Thinking about these words of wisdom I learned what I once knew, but now forgot. Applying this quote may give a boost to my life and put a smile on my face everyday.

Eden Juta

Port Washington, New York

HAPPINESS

The place to be happy is here, the time to be happy is now, the way to be happy is to make others so.

Ralph G. Ingersoll

(1833-1899)

He was a Civil War veteran, political leader and orator during the golden age of free thought. He was noted for his broad range of culture and his defense of agnosticism.

Fernando Botero

HAPPINESS

If only we'd stop trying to be happy, we could have a pretty good time.

Edith Wharton

(1866-1937)

An American author, best known for her stories and ironic novels about upper class people.

I picked this quote because it reminded me of another saying I always liked. "Just living is not enough, one must have sunshine, freedom, and a little flower." Hans Christian Andersen. Both quotes deal with happiness, and I think the point is to both recognize and find happiness in what you already have.

Therese Newman

Chicago, Illinois

HAPPINESS

Everyday happiness means getting up in the morning, you can't wait to finish your breakfast, You can't wait to do your exercises. You can't wait to put on your clothes, You can't wait to get out and you can't wait to come home, because the soup is hot.

George Burns

(1896-1996)

Born Nathan Birnbaum, he was an American comedian, actor and writer. His career spanned vaudeville, film, radio and television.

PIERRE AUGUSTE RENOIR

IMAGINATION

To know is nothing at all; to imagine is everything.

Anatole France

(1844-1924)

Born Francois-Anatole Thibault, he was a French poet, journalist and novelist.

We think we know so much!

I've tried to IMAGINE what could be

accomplished if the world was at peace

and free from hunger, poverty and cold.

Dianne Halpern

Spring Grove, Illinois

JEALOUSY

Jealousy is ugly, is bourgeois; an unworthy fuss. In jealousy there is more self-love than love.

Francois de la Rochefoucauld

(1630-1680)

A noted French author of maxims and memoirs.

Rembrandt Van Rijn

JEWISH TRADITION

The pursuit of knowledge for its own sake, an almost fanatical love of justice, and the desire for personal independence–these are the features of the Jewish tradition which make me thank my stars that I belong to it.

Albert Einstein

(1879-1955)

A German born theoretical physicist who discovered the theory of general relativity, effecting a revolution in physics.

These are the traits I have striven to live by all my life.

KNOWLEDGE is power, It enriches one's existence and well being.

JUSTICE, fairness and equal opportunity for all.

FREEDOM to have personal independence in a free society.

Edward Halpern

Spring Grove, Illinois

KINDNESS

Remember the kindness of others;
Forget your own.

Source Unknown

William-Adolphe Bouguereau

KINDNESS

I have many wonderful qualities in my life, but without kindness they are not enough.

Inspired by I Corinthians 13:3

A new testament book containing the first epistle from St. Paul to the church at Corinth.

Rembrandt Van Rijn

KINDNESS

Kind words are short and easy to speak, but their echoes are truly endless.

Mother Teresa

(1910-1997)

Born Agnes Gonxha Bojaxhiu , she was a Catholic nun of Albanian ethnicity and Indian citizenship. She won the Nobel Peace Prize in 1979 for her world wide work for the poor.

My favorite aphorism is KINDNESS by Mother Teresa. My personal feeling is when expressing kindness to another it's joyful and fulfilling from within.

Bobbet Reid, Jamaica, New York

Without much regard for context I have found this to be true. Often people acting and speaking kindly are not aware of how meaningful their actions are to those around them.

Ethan Halpern-Givens, Chicago, Illinois

Brings to mind, "Thank You," "You're Welcome," May I Help?" No Problem." Expressing and accepting appreciation is effortless, doesn't cost anything, yet makes us aware of what we do for each other.

Frances Schmidt, Port Washington, New York

KINDNESS

Having the faith to move mountains
is great, having hope in bleak circum—
stances is wonderful, but deeds of
loving kindness transform lives and
last forever.

Inspired by I Corinthians 13:2

A new testament book containing the first epistle
from St. Paul to the church at Corinth.

Kindness is a virtue that I have always respected and admired. I think about receiving kindness and giving kindness as a way of life and letting those around me know that they matter. These words are my Bible to live by.

Joan Salmon
Port Washington, New York

KINDNESS

Kindness is a language that the deaf

can hear and the blind can see.

Mark Twain

(1835-1910)

Born Samuel Langhorne Clemens he was an American author and humorist. He was best known for 'The Adventures of Huckleberry Finn.'

Kindness is the basis of many aspects of life important to me. Love, helping others, the world, the environment, practicing compassion, generosity and service. I hope this practice and ideas and actions I take will benefit not only myself and those closest to me, but also generations to come.

Shari Basom

Seattle, Washington

KINDNESS

One of the most difficult things to give away is kindness; it is usually returned.

Joseph Joubert

(1754-1824)

He was a French moralist and essayist, re membered today for his *Pensees*, published posthumously. He published nothing during his lifetime.

Mary Cassatt

KNOWLEDGE

We are drowning in information and starving for knowledge.

Rutherford D. Roger

(1921-)

Chief of personnel of the New York public library from 1954-1955. Chief of the Reference department (Later know as the Research libraries) from 1955-1957. Later on was the deputy director of the Library of Congress.

The flood of information inundating the minds of modern human beings elicits two general adaptive responses that have contrary outcomes. Many of us in our short sided panic to prevent drowning in information overload strive to master a particular small area of information, hoping our expertise will build us an island of tranquility as a refuge from the flood and then defend our achievements with violence.

The patient mind, however, realizes that the information that we choose to master must be held in a moral structure that is based on the experiential knowledge of compassion that then invites others to share in our insights and accomplishments in order to further the common good.

David Spiekerman

Seattle, Washington

KNOWLEDGE

We know lots of things we didn't use to know, but we don't know any way to prevent 'em from happening.

Will Rogers

(1879-1935)

He was an American cowboy, comedian and humorist.

I live this way-the world is such a mess, but I have all kinds of trouble finding which button to push.

Patricia Lee

Port Washington, New York

LIBERTY

If liberty means anything at all, it means the right to tell people what they do not want to hear.

George Orwell

(1903-1950)

Born Eric Arthur Blair, Orwell was an English author and journalist whose work was marked by keen intelligence and wit, a profound awarness of social justice, and an intense opposition to totalitarianism.

LIFE

The road of life can only reveal itself as it is traveled; each turn in the road reveals a surprise.

Man's future is hidden.

Source Unknown

Vincent Van Gogh

LIFE

If we had to tolerate in others all that we permit in ourselves, life would become completely unbearable.

Georges Courteline

(1858-1929)

Humor in France was known as epigram and irony, French wit was changed by delicate artists like Courteline.

Edvard Munch

LIFE

You can't do anything about the length of your life, but you can do something about its width and depth.

H. L. Mencken

(1874-1965)

Henry Louis Mencken was an American journalist, essayist, magazine editor, satirist, and an acerbic critic of American life and culture.

I went to sea for many and many years,

and loved every minute of it.

Albert S. Fialcowitz

Port Washington, New York

LIFE

Life is the art of drawing sufficient conclusions from insufficient premises.

Samuel Butler

(1835-1902)

He was an English composer, novelist and satirical author.

We are bound by traditions from other times and other cultures, and owe allegiance to any person or power greater than the Divinity manifest through our own being. Although some of the decisions we make in life are based on our cultural, spiritual, and traditional upbringing, life is basically what we make of it.

Beverly Brown
Queens, New York

LISTENING

Take time to listen, instead of waiting to talk.

Source Unknown

Hearing is a physical ability, whereas listening is actually a skill. Those of us who take the time to listen will have better success in life.

Peggy Brunner

Hollis Gardens, New York

LISTENING

One reason young children do poorly in school is that they don't listen; and the main reason they don't listen is that by the time they enter school they have conditioned themselves not to listen to adults, for most of what they hear is admonition, rebuke and nagging.

Source Unknown

I picked this aphorism because it has to do with our children and listening.

As adults, we sometimes don't show our children love and respect and how much we appreciate them.

Pauline Murphy

Brooklyn, New York

LISTENING

I think the one lesson I have learned is that there is no substitute for paying attention.

Diane Sawyer

(*1945-*)

She is the current anchor of ABC News flag-ship program, ABC World News.

LOVE

The world is not a playground, it's a schoolroom.
Life is not a holiday but an education. And the
one eternal question for us all is how better we
can love.

Henry Drummond

(1851-1897)

A scientist, evangelist and author of many books including the
multi_million seller, 'The Greatest Thing in The World' (what love
means).

LOVE

Much more genius is needed to make love than to command armies.

Ninon de Lenclos

(1620-1705)

A French author, courtesan and patron . She embodied libertinism in both theory and in practice.

LOVE

In the presence of love, miracles happen.

Robert Schuller

(1926-   )

A televangelist, he recently retired from the Crystal Cathedral mega church in Southern California.

William-Adolphe Bouguereau

LOVE

What is called 'spoiling' a child is never a symptom of love, always a substitute for love. Its object is to make the child love back the spoiling parent and this is precisely the one consequence it misses.

Sydney J. Harris

(*1917-1986*)

He was an American journalist for the Chicago Daily News and later for the Chicago Sun Times.

Pierre Auguste Renoir

LOVE

One forgives to the degree that one loves.

Francois de la Rochefoucauld

(1630-1680)

A noted French author of maxims and memoirs.

LOVE

Find something you love to do, and you'll never have to work another day in your life.

Harvey Mackay

(*1932-*)

He is the author of 4 New York Times best sellers and a nationally syndicated business columnist, as well as an accomplished speaker on business subjects.

I can attest to this. I am living proof. Love what you do and do what you love.

Kate Wilson
New York, New York

This is an ideal my grandfather taught me when I was very young and still carry it to this day. But I always took as meaning if you've got something you love with all your heart, no matter what it is you do for a paycheck, you'll always have love and happiness once you clock out.

Noah Halpern-McManus
San Francisco, California

LOVE

Life is short, and we have not too much time for gladdening the lives of those who are traveling the dark road with us. Oh, be swift to love, make haste to be kind.

Henri-Frederic Amiel

(*1821-1861*)

A Swiss philosopher, poet and critic.

I'm struck by how little time we have to see and do all we want to do and how important it is to enjoy and help others to enjoy all the wonders around us.

Betsy Budne Finnel

Port Washington, New York

LOVE

Love looks through a telescope; envy, through a telescope;
Envy, through a microscope.

Josh Billings

(1818-1885)

Was the pen name of 19th century American humorist Henry
Wheeler Shaw; the 2nd most famous humorous writer (after
Mark Twain) in the United States.

Sir John Everett Millais

LOVE

At the touch of love, everyone becomes a poet

Plato.

(429 B.C.-347 B.C.)

He was a classic Greek philosopher, mathematician, student of Socrates, writer of philosophical dialogues, and founder of the Academy in Athens.

Eric and I were touched by Plato's thoughts on love and poetry, because I am Eric's Muse and Eric is my poet. He has been writing poems for me since the day we met. We wrote this together:

Love is the constant

Life is the variable

You don't have to be perfect

To be perfectly marriable

Amy and Eric Moore
Seattle, Washington

LOVE

You are always being given opportunities to love and be loved, yet ask yourself how many times in your life you have squandered those opportunities.

Gary Zukav

His presence, humor and wisdom have inspired many to realize their soul's greatest potential. He is a master teacher and author.

I chose this aphorism because I feel that too many times in life this is true for people.

I feel that people often miss out on great love because of fear, stubbornness and stupidity and I think that is sad. I think when it comes to love, one should never squander the opportunity but always take the chance.

Leslie Mason

Long Island, New York

LOVE

In dreams and in love there are no impossibilities.

Janos Arany

(1817-1882)

He was a Hungarian writer and poet. He was often said to be the 'Shakespeare of Ballads.' He wrote more than 40 ballads which have been translated into more than 50 languages.

William-Adolphe Bouguereau

LOVE

The ultimate lesson all of us have to learn is unconditional love, which includes not only others but ourselves as well.

Elisabeth Kubler-Ross

(1926-2004)

A Swiss born psychiatrist, she was a pioneer in near death studies.

"Unconditional Love" are the words that I have felt are the wisest. They have kept me happy in the knowledge that life is NOT PERFECT. Learning to accept our own faults as well as faults in friends, family and religion. Accepting those with respect and unconditional love are the words I have lived by for almost all of my 86 years- a lesson to pass on to future generations.

Faye Schwartz
Wilmette, Illinois

LOVE

'I love you' is said every time and in every way

we show another person that he or she

is not alone.

Source Unknown

Leonardo Da Vinci

MONEY

Money may be the husk of many things, but not the kernel. It brings you food, but not appetite; medicine but not health; acquaintances, but not friends; servants, but not loyalty; days of joy, but not peace or happiness.

Henrik Ibsen
(1828-1906)

A major 19 th century Norwegian playwright, theater director and poet. He is often referred to as 'The Father' of modern theater.

Jules Grun

MONEY

Money is a guarantee that we may have what we want in the future. Though we need nothing at the moment, it insures the possibility of satisfying a necessary desire when it arises.

Aristotle

(384 B.C.-322 B.C.)

A Greek philosopher, a student of Plato, and a teacher of Alexander the Great.

MONEY

If money is not thy servant, it will be thy master.
The covetous man cannot so properly be said
to possess wealth, as that may be said to
possess him.

Francis Bacon
(1561-1626)

He was an English philosopher, statesman, scientist, lawyer,
jurist, author and father of the Scientific Method.

Quinten Metsys

MONEY

If you want to feel rich, just count all the things

you have that money can't buy.

Source Unknown

I try to be happy in my own life, as I live it day to day. Some of the things that I am richest in are that I am loved, I can see the sun out of my window or feel it on my face as I step outside. I have family and friends, work I love and a warm place to come home to. I can assist others. These are priceless.

Lindsey Halpern-Givens
Crystal Lake, Illinois

The mutual love and respect of family are the greatest assets one can own.

Larry Stein
Montville, New Jersey

PEACE

Peace is a state of mind. It is the freedom from all desire to be secure.

Indian proverb

I chose this because I have found myself at times being in a place of wanting to feel more secure. Secure and protected from a loved one's illness, financial worries or relational conflict, to name a few.

This is usually a place that is full of anxiety, doubt and discontent. The desire to be more secure is a desire , in my observation, that if it becomes unbalanced leads us to blindly grasp on to limiting beliefs and ideology.

It can be a destructive force within an individual, and in relationships, which of course leads us away from peace.

Nicole Falcone
S. Hadley, Massachusetts

PEACE

I can have peace of mind only when I forgive rather than judge.

Gerald Jampolsky

He is a psychiatrist formerly on the faculty of the University of California medical center in San Francisco. He is the co-founder of the Jampolsky Outreach Foundation.

Hans Memling

PEACE

There never was a good war, or a bad peace.

Benjamin Franklin

(1706-1790)

He was an American scientist, inventor, statesman, printer and philosopher.

Although we were taught to refer to World War II as 'good war' due to the necessity to defeat the extremely evil forces of the Nazis, I wish for the future that we will find other alternatives to war as a means of solving the conflicts that arise in the world.
We know now with our modern technology we can destroy the planet and all life on it. Therefore we must find a way to peace for the sake of survival.

Nettie Jonath

Port Washington, New York

RELATIONSHIPS

One plus one equals three. The man, the woman, and the relationship.

Source Unknown

Jean-Antoine Watteau

RELIGION

The test of any person's religion is not how you treat God, but how you treat people.

Source Unknown

Vincent Van Gogh

RELIGION

People calling themselves Christians

(or whatever) are not necessarily religious.

Source Unknown

Velasquez El Greco

RELIGION

The Bible didn't cause wars; men do.

Source Unknown

RELIGION

A belief is not necessarily anything else but a sense of awe and wonder about something.

Source Unknown

SACRIFICE

The important thing is to be able at any moment to sacrifice what we are for what we could be.

Charles DuBos

(1882-1939)

He was the French critic of French and English literature. He was the real author of this aphorism, not Charles DuBois.

Winslow Homer

SUCCESS

For an actress to be a success she must have the face of Venus, the brains of Minerva, the grace of Terpsichore, the memory of Macaulay, the figure of Juno, and the hide of a rhinoceros.

Ethel Barrymore

(1879-1959)

She was an American actress, and a member of the Barrymore family of actors.

Pierre Auguste Renoir

SUCCESS

As soon as you trust yourself, you will know how to live.

Johann Wolfgang Von Goethe

(1749-1832)

He was considered the supreme genius of modern German literature, side by side with Schiller. His work spans the fields of poetry, drama, literature, philosophy and science.

As a young adult in the midst of making life changing decisions a quote like this is a guiding star. Being able to rely on my gut instincts is a trait my mother has instilled in me from a very young age. It has proven to be one of my most reliable skills. Thank you mom.

Annabel Neff, San Francisco, California

As a recent college graduate trying to find my way in life, trusting myself-having confidence in my abilities and the fact that everything will work out all right-is one of the hardest things for me. And knowing how to live? The concept is beyond foreign. It almost seems too simple and the path ahead no less daunting. But maybe I should forget the 'how to live' part and just start by trusting myself. I guess that's Goethe's point; you don't need a vision for the future, just the confidence to move towards it.

Katie Mancher, Port Washington, New York

SUCCESS

We are prone to judge success by the index

of our salaries or the size of our automobiles

rather than by the quality of our service

and our relationship to mankind.

Dr. Martin Luther King Jr.

(1929-1968)

He was born Michael, but later had his name changed to Martin.
He graduated from high school at the age of fifteen; won the
Nobel Peace Prize in 1964.

Tamara de Lempicka

SUCCESS

Success is a consequence and must not be a goal.

Gustave Flaubert

(1826-1880)

A French writer who is counted among the greatest Western novelists. He is known especially for his first novel, 'Madame Bovary.'

Antoine Vollon

SUCCESS

The greatest barrier to success is the fear of failure.

Sven-Goran Eriksson

(1948-)

He is a Swedish football manager. He is the only manager to win league-and-cup doubles in three different countries; England, Mexico and Cote D'Ivoire.

I like this aphorism because it reminds me of myself. For me, fear is the reason that when we really try hard we do our best to succeed.

Nadira Caprietta Elliott

Rosedale, New York

TODAY

Today is the tomorrow you worried about

yesterday-but it never happened.

Source Unknown

How true this is! I learned long ago that worry doesn't accomplish anything positive.

What it does produce is negative stress. I need to remind myself of this truth continually.

TODAY is the day the LORD has made. Let us rejoice and be glad in it.

Joan Gerken
Port Washington, New York

"Source unknown" could very well have been my wise husband of 61 years who tells me this all the time. I DO listen to him and I really DO try, but must admit to still having many sleepless nights .

Betty Newman
Floral Park, New York

TOLERANCE

Tolerance is another word for indifference.

William Somerset Maugham

(1874-1965)

He was an English playwright, novelist and short story writer. He was among the most popular writers of his era.

TRUTH

Skepticism is the first step toward truth.

Denis Diderot

(1713-1784)

A French philosopher, art critic and writer, he was a prominent 'persona' during the Enlightenment. He was best know as co- founder and chief editor and contributor to the 'Encyclopedie.'

Skepticism communicates a willingness to admit so many qualities- humility, thoughtfulness, eagerness-that fulfill and inform life. Pausing to consider that I do not know everything, about the world or myself, allows me to appreciate that there is always something more I can improve, appreciate, and question. Truth requires work, and skepticism is the tool that lets us approach truth.

Josh Halpern-Givens
Sycamore, Illinois

TRUTH

Speak the truth, but leave immediately after.

Slovenian Proverb

Thomas Rowlandson

TRUTH

To express unafraid and unashamed what one really thinks and feels is one of the great consolations of life.

Theodor Reik
(1888-1969)

Born in Vienna, he was a prominent psychoanalyst who trained with Freud.

Fernando Botero

TRUTH

There are two mistakes one can make along the road to truth; not going all the way, and not starting.

Buddha

(565 B.C.- 483 B.C.)

Siddartha Gautama was a spiritual teacher who founded Buddhism. He is the supreme Buddha of our age meaning 'awakened one' or the 'enlightened one.'

As a scientist, I try to seek the truth in earthly processes and in doing so, see their beauty all the clearer. When studying and exploring nature 'going all the way' can quickly become overwhelming as it tends to lead to more questions than answers.

Seemingly insurmountable questions may discourage one from ever starting, but to get anywhere, every last person must at least start.

Shannon McCarragher
Sycamore, Illinois

TRUTH

We don't see things as they are; we see them as
we are.

Anais Nin

(1903-1977)

A French-Cuban author, based first in France and later in the
U.S., she became famous for her published journals.

Amedeo Modigliani

TRUTH

If one tells the truth, one is sure, sooner or later, to be found out.

Oscar Wilde

(1854-1900)

He was an Irish writer and poet, one of London's most popular playwrights in the early 1890s. Remembered for his epigrams, plays and the circumstances of his imprisonment , followed by his early death.

unknown. *Portrait of Nostradamus*

VIRTUE

Virtue is not hereditary.

Thomas Paine

(1737-1809)

He was an author, pamphleteer, inventor, intellect and revolutionary. A radical protagonist, he was the voice of the common man.

Leonardo Da Vinci

WISDOM

We don't receive wisdom; we must discover it for ourselves after a journey that no one can take for us or spare us.

Marcel Proust

(1871-1922)

A French intellectual, novelist, essayist and critic; best known for his work, 'Remembrance of Things Past.'

This quote is a great reminder that there is no form of education or indoctrination that can supplant life experience. Education helps guide us in our journey and how to focus our ideas, but one can only learn and understand by doing. I find this to be true as I continue to learn and grow everyday.

Johanna Berger
Pasadena, California

WISDOM

I do not believe in the collective wisdom of individual ignorance.

Thomas Carlyle

(1795-1881)

He was a Scottish satirical writer, essayist, historian and teacher. During the Victorian era he became a controversial social commentator.

This is an aphorism for our time, commenting on the dependence in today's political world on public opinion surveys. These surveys too often take seriously as collective wisdom the opinions of many ignorant individuals.

Rhoda Selvin

Port Washington, New York

WISDOM

Be not afraid of growing slowly; be afraid only of standing still.

Chinese Proverb

A lesson for older Americans: To stay young and grow you have to be open to change or your limited life span will pass you by.

Lucille Stein

Montville, New Jersey

WISDOM

Men in general judge more from appearances than from reality. All men have eyes, but few have the gift of penetration.

Niccolo Machiavelli

(1469-1527)

He was an Italian philosopher, humanist and writer who lived in Florence during the Renaissance.

Rembrandt Van Rijn

WISDOM

Time is a great teacher, but unfortunately it kills all its pupils.

Hector Berlioz

(1803-1869)

A Frenchman, not only was he one of the most original of the great composers, but was also an innovator as a practical musician.
He was a writer and a critic whose literary achievement was hardly less significant than his musical output.

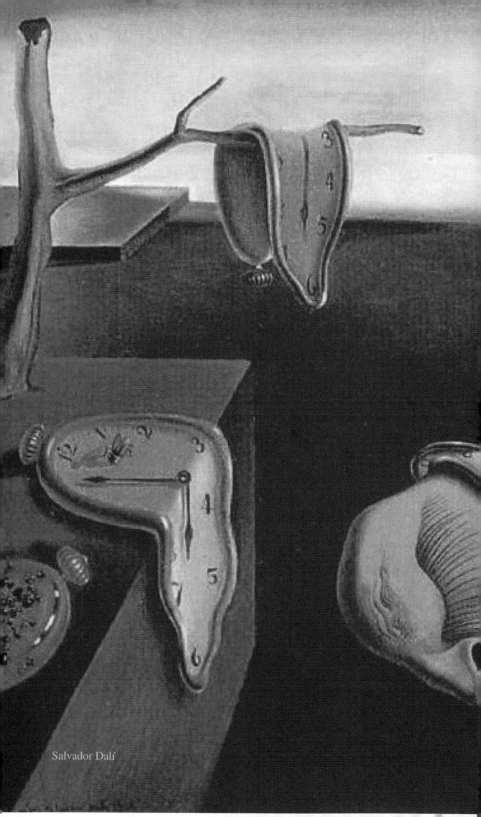

Salvador Dalí

WISDOM

Knowledge comes, but wisdom lingers.

Lord Alfred Tennyson

(1809- 1892)

An English poet often regarded as the chief representative of the Victorian age in poetry. He succeeded Wordsworth as Poet Laureate in 1850.

Rembrandt Van Rijn

WORDS TO LIVE BY

Here are 7 different "Old Sayings"
that are probably not aphorisms.

In my opinion, these are thought provokers.

LOVE

Love that is hoarded moulds at last
Until we know someday
The only thing we ever have
Is what we give away.

Louis Ginsberg
(1896-1976)

He was a poet, English teacher and Socialist.
He was the father of Allen Ginsberg.

LOVE

Do remember–to forget
Anger, worry, and regret.
Love while you've got love to give
Live while you've got life to live.

Piet Hein
(1905-1996)

A Danish scientist, mathematician, inventor, designer, author and poet. He often wrote under the Norse pseudonym 'Kumbel' mean–ing tombstone.

EGO

EGOIST-

I'm an important part of the world.

EGOTIST-

The world revolves around me.

WHICH are you?

Source Unknown

IDENTITY

Who am I?

What am I like (as a person)?

How do I fit into the world?

Source Unknown

RECTITUDE

These days, rectitude is the only non
conformity. Heroic is the man who
dares to be legitimate. Perhaps we
are unaware of it ourselves, but even
though everything we understand as
principle and decency is so much dis_
credited these days we still feel a need
for it.

Crebillion Fils
(1707-1777)

He was a French novelist, short story writer and
dramatist. His real name was
Claude Prosper Jolyot de (fils).

SUCCESS

What is success? To laugh often and love much, to win the respect of in- telligent persons and the affection of children; to earn the approbation of honest critics and endure the betrayal of false friends; to appreciate beauty; to find the best in others; to give one's self; to leave the world a bit better, whether by a healthy child, a garden patch or a redeemed social condition; to have played and laughed with enthusiasm and sung with exaltation; to know even one life has breathed easier because you have lived_this is to have succeeded.

Ralph Waldo Emerson
(1803-1882)

He was an American lecturer, philosopher, essayist and poet. He was best remembered for leading the Transcendentalist movement of the mid 19th century.

Twenty years ago, reading this verse changed my life. I felt free, deeply moved and acknowledged for my values and my life's work! Thank you Ralph Waldo Emerson for having touched one life. I do breathe a little easier.

Mara Halpern

Sunderland, Massachusetts

VIRTUE

To love means to love the unlovable
To forgive means to forgive the un-
forgivable
To have faith means believing the
unbelievable
Hope is to hope when things are
hopeless
Or else they're not virtues at all.

G.K Chesterton
(1874-1936)

An Englishman, he was equally at ease with social
criticism, history, politics, economics, philosophy and
theology. His style was marked by humility,
consistency, paradox, wit and wonder.

NOTES

NOTES

5092194R00119

Made in the USA
San Bernardino, CA
23 October 2013